# BLITZ

## Terry Deary
### Illustrated by Mike Phillips

Scholastic Children's Books,
Euston House, 24 Eversholt Street,
London, NW1 1DB, UK

A division of Scholastic Ltd
London ~ New York ~ Toronto ~ Sydney ~ Auckland
Mexico City ~ New Delhi ~ Hong Kong

First published in the UK by Scholastic Ltd, 2009
(as Horrible Histories Handbooks: Blitz)
This edition published 2010

Text copyright © Terry Deary, 2009
Cover illustration copyright © Martin Brown, 2009
Inside illustrations by Mike Phillips, based on the style of the
original *Horrible Histories* artwork by Martin Brown
Illustrations copyright © Mike Phillips, 2009
All rights reserved

ISBN 978 1407 11749 2

Printed and bound by Tien Wah Press Pte. Ltd, Malaysia

2 4 6 8 10 9 7 5 3 1

The right of Terry Deary, Martin Brown and Mike Phillips to be identified as the author and
illustrators of this work respectively has been asserted by them in accordance with the Copyright,
Designs and Patents Act, 1988.

# INTRODUCTION

The Second World War was a different sort of war for the British people. In a popular wartime film a vicar summed it up:

> *This is not only a war of soldiers in uniforms. It is a war of the people - and it must be fought not only on the battlefields but in the cities and villages, in the factories and on the farms, in the homes and in the heart of every man, woman and child who loves freedom. Well, we have buried our dead but we shall not forget them. Instead they will inspire us with an unbreakable determination to free ourselves and those who come after us from the tyranny and terror that threaten to strike us down. This is a people's war. It is our war. We are the fighters.*

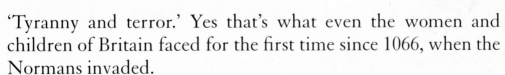

'Tyranny and terror.' Yes that's what even the women and children of Britain faced for the first time since 1066, when the Normans invaded.

This was nothing new for the rest of the world, of course. Millions of families had been caught up in wars of terror in the past. Warriors know that a good way to win a war quickly is to scare the enemy so badly they give up!

In the 1930s Mr Hitler and his German armies came up with the idea of 'Blitzkrieg' … it means 'Lightning War'. General Guderian told the German army how to beat Poland…

WE HIT THEM WITH THOUSANDS OF BOMBS FROM THE AIR AND SMASH THEIR DEFENCES. THEN WE SEND IN TANKS. WE KNOCK THEM OUT BEFORE THEY KNOW WHAT HAS HIT THEM!

BOOOM!

BRRUM! BRRUM!

POLAND

Poland was as good as beaten. Hitler turned on France and Britain went to help. The Brits were driven back home.

Time to hit Britain with a Blitzkrieg. And as General Guderian would say, you keep hitting them till they give in!

THE DEFEATED ENEMY MUST BE GIVEN NO PEACE

The German bombers arrived over London and the Blitz began.

Would Britain survive? Would YOU survive?

What you need are some top tips to help you decide. A sort of handbook to help you through the times of terror. And, as it happens, you are holding one in your grubby hands right now!

Read on and live … or put the book back on the shelf and suffer…

# TERRIBLE TIMELINE

## 10 JULY 1940

The German air force (Luftwaffe) starts its mass bomber attacks on British factories and airfields. In the next three months the British Royal Air Force (RAF) will lose 792 planes and over 500 pilots will be killed. This time will become known as the 'Battle of Britain'.

## 24 AUGUST 1940

The German air force drops bombs on Birmingham and Liverpool. They aim to sink ships and wreck docks and factories … but they miss. They hit houses and kill ordinary people. Welcome to the war! So…

## 25 AUGUST 1940

… the RAF drops bombs on ordinary German people. German leader Adolf Hitler is furious. He says…

> *I want attacks on the people and air defences of large British cities, including London, by day and night.*

## 7 SEPTEMBER 1940

The day when MOST people say the Blitz starts. The German air force starts bombing London at night. On the first day this

Blitz kills 430 people and 1,600 more are badly injured. The German bombers will be back the next day and another 412 will die. RAF fighter pilots try to shoot down the bombers.

### 31 OCTOBER 1940

The day historians say the Battle of Britain ends … but the Blitz goes on, night after night, for 57 nights.

### 29 DECEMBER 1940

A massive raid. The night that is known as 'The Second Great Fire of London'.

### 3 MAY 1941

A large bomb on Liverpool docks sets fire to a ship called the Malakand … which is loaded with bombs! Bits of the ship are found nearly three miles away.

### 10 MAY 1941

The day known as 'The darkest hour' when over 1,500 people die in London.

### FEBRUARY 1942

The RAF stops aiming for German factory targets and starts aiming to wipe out the homes of 'workers' … families in other words.

### APRIL 1942

So Germany does the same, tit-for-tat. A German book called The Baedeker Tourist Guide to Britain shows Britain's favourite tourist cities. A Nazi writer, Baron Gustav Braun von Sturm, says:

*We shall go out and bomb every building in Britain marked with three stars in the Baedeker Guide.*

The cities attacked are Exeter, Bath, Norwich, York and Canterbury.

## 22 AUGUST 1942

A British spy in Denmark finds a new German flying bomb. It crashes while being tested. These 'V1' flying bombs could win the war for Germany.

## MAY 1943

Brit leader Winston Churchill orders 'Operation Crossbow', a plan to wreck the V1 launch sites. But 36,000 tons of Brit bombs fail to stop the V1s.

## 21 JANUARY 1944

The 'Baby Blitz' starts with a raid on London. The Luftwaffe aren't very good at hitting their targets now. They lose lots of planes and drop very few bombs. The Baby Blitz ends in May 1944.

## 12 JUNE 1944

New terror weapon: the V1 bombs begin to rain on Britain. First one lands and people panic. Over a million people flee London.

## 8 SEPTEMBER 1944

Now a faster, bigger flying bomb, the V2, arrives.

## 27 MARCH 1945

The V2 attacks stop when British soldiers capture the launch sites.

## APRIL 1945

End of the war. Bombing has killed 60,595 British people and taken between 305,000 and 600,000 German lives. Britain has been Blitzed – but Germany has been flattened.

## 30 APRIL 1945

Big Ben is lit up – the sign that the Blackout in Britain has ended five years and 123 days since it dimmed Blitzed Britain.

## 6 AUGUST 1945

Japan has carried on fighting … so the US Air Force 'blitzes' Hiroshima and (three days later) Nagasaki. The atomic bombs are so powerful it takes just one on each city to wipe them out.

# THE FABULOUS FEW

The British Prime Minister during World War II is Winston Churchill. When the German air force (Luftwaffe) tries to smash Britain, the British Royal Air Force fights back. This 'Battle of Britain' goes on from 10 July to 31 October 1940.

'Winnie' says…

*Never in the field of human conflict was so much owed by so many to so few.*

## Pilot problems

The 'few' are 1,103 pilots on 1 July 1940.

They are fighting two enemies: the Luftwaffe … and the Royal Air Force – their own commanders.

The RAF commanders tell their pilots:

The flight leader at the front can look out for enemy planes. But the other 11 pilots can't.

So the German pilots can swoop down and shoot the RAF pilots who aren't able to look out. The Germans call them…

The rows of idiots change their shape…

DON'T FLY SO CLOSE. AND HAVE A COUPLE OF 'WEAVERS' AT THE BACK ON LOOKOUT. GOOD JOB FOR THE YOUNG PILOTS…

BUT, SIR…

DON'T ARGUE! I FOUGHT IN THE FIRST WORLD WAR, YOU KNOW!

YES, SIR

The young pilots at the back – the 'weavers' – are usually the first to die.

AFTER the Battle of Britain the RAF changes the rules to copy the German way of fighting.

A BIT LATE FOR ME!

ONE OF THE FEW DIED JULY 1940

**Dodgy death toll**

The British and the Germans lie about how many enemy planes they have shot down and how many they have lost. Old Henry V had done the same at Agincourt…

THERE ARE 10,000 FRENCH DEAD AND JUST 29 ENGLISH

BRILLIANT!

NOT IF YOU'RE ONE OF THE 29, MATE!

It was nonsense. But people are still fibbing 600 years later.

18 August 1940 has been called 'The Hardest Day' when each side loses a lot of planes and pilots. But how many? There are THREE lots of facts … who do you believe?

### RAF COMMANDER

144 German planes shot down

23 Brit planes shot down … we won by 121

### GERMAN COMMANDER

36 German planes shot down

147 Brit planes shot down … we won by 111

### HORRIBLY TRUE HISTORIAN

READ ALL ABOUT IT!

69 German planes shot down

68 Brit planes shot down … it's almost a draw!

The Horrible Historian, of course!

Five hundred and forty-four British pilots lose their lives trying to stop the Luftwaffe. But they win. If they had lost then Germany would have tried to invade.

The BAD news is that the Germans turn their bombers on London instead.

On 7 September 1940 the Blitz starts for real.

---

### ☠ DID YOU KNOW…? ☠

The German air force refuse to give their Messerschmitt fighter planes extra fuel tanks. So some pilots run out of petrol and land in the English Channel. The plane is lost, the pilot drowns. Potty.

# BOMB-SPOTTING

Know your enemy, they say. So if you want to survive the Blitz get to know these blitzing bombs.

If you are close enough to spot a bomb then you'll probably be dead a few seconds later. So spot these bombs ... then duck!

## High explosive

A big bang that blasts down walls, wrecks water pipes, gas pipes and electric cables and makes holes in the road so rescue vehicles can't get to the fires and the victims.

## Magnesium incendiary bombs

They land and start burning fiercely. Very hard to put out the fires.

## Petrol incendiary bombs

Spread flaming petrol over a wide area so there's less chance of escape.

## High-explosive parachute air- mines

They float down, explode in the air and blow the roofs off buildings. That way the next lot of incendiary bombs will fall INSIDE buildings, not just on the roof tiles.

## Petrol incendiary parachute air mines

Float down and spray flaming petrol on the buildings, people, cars (and cats and dogs) below.

## Flares

They float slowest of all and burn brightly. Enemy aircraft can see them from miles away and the light shows them where to drop their bombs.

## V1 flying bomb

The 'Vergeltung' 1 bomb ... and that means 'Revenge'. It flies off a sort of ski-slope launcher.

## V2 rocket bomb

Bigger, faster and nastier than the V1. They go 50 miles high so there's no stopping them.

INCENDIARY BOMB

PARACHUTE AIR-MINE

V1 FLYING BOMB

V2 FLYING BOMB

Beware! Not all Blitzed Brit bombs are dropped by Germans from the sky. In big cities like Liverpool, Birmingham and London people might go to the cinema or the market and a fire bomb goes off in the middle of a crowd. German spies? No. Irish rebels trying to panic people.

Do they panic? One report says FOUR fire bombs went off in a Birmingham cinema. Three hundred people rushed to the doors but one man stood up and cried…

The fires fizzled out, the smoke cleared and the people finished watching the film. Un-bothered Brits.

## Toilet terror

In Liverpool a man goes to the toilet and leaves the lid up. Minutes later an incendiary bomb goes through the roof and lands straight in the toilet. It sizzles and spits in the water but the house is saved.

Sadly the toilet can't be saved and it goes to that great bathroom in the sky.

Anti-aircraft guns make houses shake. One council tries to ban them because they are cracking toilet bowls.

# BAD BLACKOUT

The enemy bombers can't blitz you if they can't see you! So, turn out all the lights – or hide them behind thick curtains – and hope the bombers give up and go home. Nice idea.

Britain has 'The blackout'.

Here are ten things they never tell you...

**1** There is never a full blackout.

Cinemas and restaurants can light up their signs until an air-raid warning sounds.

Councils can have faint street lighting (called 'glimmer' lighting) at dangerous spots like crossroads.

In November 1939 the government says churches may have some light.

**2** Cars, buses and lorries drive with the help of feeble little side lights. There are thousands of accidents. The king's doctor,

Wilfred Trotter, says…

*The Luftwaffe are frightening the British into blackout rules. They are able to kill 600 people a month without ever taking to the air, and it costs Germany exactly nothing.*

The government has to change the law. They let motors drive with headlamps that have covers with three slits in. It isn't much better!

**3** The government comes up with an idea to help drivers see their way in the dark: they paint white lines down the middle of the road … and we still have them.

They also have car bumpers painted white so people walking on the road can see what is just about to kill them.

**4** Torches are banned at the start of the war. But people DO start to carry torches in the blackout. A little rhyme is written to help people remember the rules, called 'Billy Brown's Highway Code'.

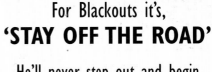

For Blackouts it's,
## 'STAY OFF THE ROAD'

He'll never step out and begin
To meet a bus that's pulling in.

He doesn't wave his torch at night,
But 'flags' his bus with something white.

He never jostles in a queue
But waits and takes his turn. Do you?

The government gives people torches to be safer in the dark ... but very few can find the right batteries. They just go on wandering in the dark, getting run over.

I THOUGHT THAT WAS OUR JOB?

EEEK!

**5** A man drops his false teeth in the street. He strikes a match to look for them. He is fined ten shillings for showing a light in the blackout. (We don't know if he ever finds the teeth. Sorry.)

**6** Cars are not allowed to drive faster than 20 miles an hour at night. Cheerful posters showing road deaths are pasted on walls.

IT WASN'T FAR... JUST A FEW YARDS ACROSS THE ROAD. HE WANTED TO CATCH THE BUS, SO HE TOOK A CHANCE AND RAN FOR IT.

DEATH HAPPENED TO GET IN HIS WAY!

PUT THAT LIGHT OUT!

Death 'happened to get in his way'? Death ... driving a ten-ton truck.

**7** Pedestrians are knocked down and killed by cars and lorries in the blackout. We know that. But pedestrians are also being knocked down and killed by other pedestrians! There's a new rule:

# KEEP LEFT ON THE PAVEMENT

**8** George Lovell puts up his blackout curtains. He goes outside to check if there is any light showing. There is! A warden is walking past and arrests George. He is fined.

**9** A garage owner switches on a light and he is fined. So what? It is the middle of the day!

**10** Horrible Histories quick question: In September 1944 bombing raids have stopped. The blackout is replaced with what?
   a) The light-up
   b) The floodlight-up
   c) The dim-out

**Answer:**
c) The dim-out allows towns to be lit dimly – about the same light you'd get from the moon.

# HELTER SHELTER

If bombs are going to fall, you need a shelter to survive. If thousands of bombs are going to fall, you need thousands of shelters ... and they have to be cheap and simple to make.

**Anderson shelters**

Yes, the trick is to get to a shelter on time. But what sort of shelter?

In 1938 Sir John Anderson invents a cheap shelter that's quick to build. Any fool can put it up ... even a teacher!

PLANT YOUR GARDEN ONTO THE SHELTER ROOF. PLANT VEGETABLES AND FLOWERS

PUT IN CHAIRS, BEDS AND, OF COURSE, A POTTY TO PEE AND POO IN ... HERE'S ONE I DID EARLIER...

**Quick quiz:**

How does Sir John Anderson test his Anderson shelter?

a) He drops a bomb on it.

b) He drives a tank over it.

c) He jumps up and down on it.

**Answer:**

c) He jumps on the roof of one ... which is not quite as deadly as a German bomb, of course. The shelter survives, and so does Sir John.

**Morrison shelters**

Don't have a garden? Never mind, a government minister called Herbert Morrison has come up with the 'Morrison shelter' ... wonder where he got the name from?

It is like a heavy steel table and you can put it in your living room. You can sleep under there with another couple of people ... if you can stand the smell.

It will save you from being crushed if your house is bombed ... but you will have to wait for someone to come and dig you out.

## Tube stations

In London the Tube stations make great places to shelter, don't they? Deep underground with several ways to get in and out.

The Minister of Home Security, Herbert Morrison, says...

NO! THERE ARE NO TOILETS IN TUBE STATIONS. YOU WILL GET DISEASES AND DIE! YOU MAY FALL ON THE LINES. YOU MAY WANT TO GO HOME!

The people go into the Tube stations anyway! The government has to change its mind.

ON THE OTHER HAND, MAYBE IT'S NOT SUCH A BAD IDEA AFTER ALL!

Seventy-nine stations are fitted with bunk-beds for 22,000 people and have smelly chemical toilets. (Some just have smelly buckets that get kicked over ... phew!)

They have 124 canteens with smelly food.

Each shelter has a marshal...

GET ON YER HORSE AND GET OUTTA TOWN, COWBOY!

NOT *THAT* SORT OF MARSHAL, STUPID! SOMEONE IN CHARGE

## Posh protection

As usual it is the poor people who suffer the worst in a war. The rich run off to their country houses or country hotels. Posh clubs in London have special comfy cellars for their rich members.

The government says...

> WE DON'T WANT TOO MANY DEEP SHELTERS. PEOPLE MAY GO DOWN THERE AND NEVER COME OUT!

No deep shelters then? Where do the government workers go when there is a raid?

The government has the old Down Street tube station (between Piccadilly and Hyde Park on the Piccadilly line) fitted out as a shelter. A DEEP shelter. It has bathrooms, offices and bedrooms. It's still there - dusty and forgotten.

There are no bathrooms and bedrooms for the rest of the Blitzed Brits.

## Not-so-super shelters

Of course some shelters are about as useful as an old umbrella...

## Terrible Tubes

The Tube stations are not always safe … but the government keeps quiet about the deaths till after the war…

**TUBE TERMINALS**

17 September 1940 - Direct hit on Marble Arch tube station - 20 dead

14 October 1940 - Balham tube station, bomb hits water and sewage pipes - 68 dead

11 January 1941 - Direct hit at Bank where the road above collapses - 56 dead

## Grim Bethnal Green

But it isn't just enemy bombs that can kill you.

In 1943 the German air force starts 'hit-and-run' raids – they were called 'tip and run' at the time – fast bombing that kills people before they have a chance to get to shelters.

On 4 March 1943 there are 500 people sheltering for the night in Bethnal Green Underground station. Then comes a hit-and-run panic…

AT QUARTER PAST EIGHT THE AIR-RAID SIREN SOUNDED. HUNDREDS OF PEOPLE RAN FROM THEIR HOMES TO BETHNAL GREEN STATION

WAAA

PEOPLE RAN FROM CINEMAS – BUSES STOPPED TO LET PASSENGERS ENTER THE SHELTER

SUDDENLY THE LONDON GUNNERS SENT 60 ROCKETS UP TO HIT THE GERMAN BOMBERS. THE NOISE WAS TERRIFYING

BOOM!

IN JUST TEN MINUTES 1,500 PEOPLE TRIED TO JAM INTO THE TUBE TUNNEL

ONE WOMAN WITH A CHILD IN HER ARMS TUMBLED. A MAN TRIPPED OVER HER, OTHERS SLIPPED AND THE CROWD BEHIND BEGAN FALLING ON TOP OF ONE ANOTHER

IN JUST 15 SECONDS THE STAIRS WERE JAMMED WITH HUNDREDS OF PEOPLE

173 PEOPLE – 84 WOMEN, 62 CHILDREN AND 27 MEN – WERE CRUSHED OR SUFFOCATED IN THIS TERRIBLE ACCIDENT

KILLED BY FRIENDS' FEET, THE MOST HORRIBLE SHELTER DEATHS OF ALL

There was just one small 25-watt light bulb to light the stairs.

**Factory fizz**

Many houses and factories have cellars. A good place to hide when bombs start to fall? Not always.

Wilkinson's Lemonade factory in North Shields is hit on 3 May 1941. One hundred and seven workers flee to the basement. But a bomb makes the ceiling collapse and the heavy lemonade bottle machines fall on them.

Pop!

### Street shelters

These are built from March 1940. They are made with thick brick walls, a concrete roof and about ten little rooms with six bunks in each.

NOT WHAT YOU'D CALL A ROOM WITH A VIEW, THEN?

In one town a bomb bursts a water pipe and floods the shelter. The corridors are too narrow to escape from and the people inside drown.

NO, MORE LIKE A TOMB WITH A VIEW!

Street shelters are never popular after that. People like their own garden shelters.

### Railway arches

If a bridge is tough enough to carry a train it can keep off a bomb, can't it?

Hmmm! In Liverpool hundreds of people shelter underneath the railway arches at Bentinck Street.

A bomb blows the bridge apart and hundreds die.

A popular song of the 1930s was called 'Underneath the Arches'…

*Underneath the arches, I dream my dreams away.*
*Underneath the arches, On cobblestones I lay.*
*Pavement is my pillow, No matter where I stray.*
*Underneath the arches, I dream my dreams away.*

Or, in Bentinck Street, 'Underneath the arches, my brains get blown away.'

## Best bomb shelter?

Liverpool is shattered by many bombing raids. But one place seems to get lucky … Liverpool Cathedral.

• A high-explosive bomb goes clean through the roof, but it hits a beam and bounces back out. It explodes in the street. Cathedral windows are blown out but the building survives.

• In another raid a large bomb lands bang on the cathedral steps … or not-bang on the cathedral steps, because it fails to go off. The cathedral survives … again. Holy smoke.

The Archbishop of Liverpool says…

*Liverpool has been tried by fire, it has faced the might of airborne Germany, and Merseyside has won.*

But 550 Liverpool corpses are placed in a common grave in Anfield cemetery. They are the 'Unknown Warriors of The Battle of Britain' … so not everyone on Merseyside 'has won'.

# EVIL FOR EVACUEES

I f big cities are being bombed then we have to save the children. It is the children who can grow up to become soldiers ... and get shot in another war. So how do we save the children?

Send them into the countryside – the enemy can't Blitz every little village in Britain, can they?

The children are 'evacuated' and are known as evacuees. Sir John Anderson, who is in charge of the plan, has decided that people living in the country will be forced to take in these evacuees. The people who take in evacuees are known as 'billetors'.

### Cruel for kids

It isn't a lot of fun being taken from your home and dumped in a strange town in the country. You might be lucky and get a good 'billetor' ... or the billetors might not want you at all if you're a bit scruffy or rough!

One evacuee said…

*We were herded like cattle around the streets of Oswestry. They knocked on the doors of the billetors who said they wanted an evacuee. The billetors came out of their houses and picked the ones they liked the look of. It was total chaos. Some children were still being walked around the streets at midnight.*

## ☠ DID YOU KNOW…? ☠

A billetor will be paid ten shillings and six pence a week to look after an evacuee. If you take more than one then you get eight shillings and six pence for each extra one.

• Some evacuees go home … but the country house owners still claim the money. Naughty.

• Some house owners fill in the forms and take the money for children who never exist! That's cheating.

## ☠ DID YOU ALSO KNOW…? ☠

The government can't send ALL the London children into the countryside. They send the children from the poorest slums. One nutty reason given by the government is…

*The poor are most likely to be driven mad with fright and cause panic in the streets.*

## Lovable lice and lousy language

Some evacuees come from city slums and are not very clean. They bring 'friends' with them. 'Friends' that crawl over their scalps or under their skin!

• Around half of the evacuated children have fleas or head-lice. It is said some country folk try to get rid of lice by using sheep-dip on children's heads! Baa-ad idea.

• Other children have impetigo and scabies, which make them itch.

YOU USUALLY FIND IMPETIGO AROUND THE NOSE AND MOUTH AND HANDS. IT BEGINS AS TINY BLISTERS THAT BURST AND LEAVE SMALL WET PATCHES OF RED SKIN THAT MAY LEAK FLUID. THEN A YELLOWISH-BROWN CRUST COVERS THE AREA, MAKING IT LOOK LIKE IT HAS BEEN COATED WITH HONEY OR BROWN SUGAR

SWEET!

But the scabs don't taste like honey or brown sugar so don't lick them.

Billetors were sometimes horrified by the behaviour of the evacuees.
• Out of every 20 evacuees one will not have been trained to use the toilet – even if they are eleven years or older.
One six-year-old arrives at his new home and starts to poo in the middle of the living room.
His mother screams at him…

YOU DIRTY THING, MESSING UP THE LADY'S CARPET! GO AND DO IT IN THE CORNER!

• Many evacuees have problems with bed-wetting at night while others don't know how a flushing toilet works.

• One child doesn't like clean white sheets ... they are 'for dead people'.

• Some little girls have never worn knickers and other children have never seen pyjamas.

• Some like to use some shocking swear words they learned back home.

• Some evacuees are caught peeling off wallpaper. They are looking for insects, the way they do back home in the slums.

• Some bring bad little habits to the country – shop-lifting and pick-pocketing.

**Terror for tiny townies**
Would YOU like to have some scruffy kid forced to share your house? Not everyone likes the idea. Who could the country people take revenge on?

Sir John Anderson? No. The little evacuees. There are thousands of happy tales ... but thousands of terror tales too...

> *I was so miserable I tried to cut my own throat ... but the knife was blunt.*

> *I was beaten at least once a week with a stick, a poker, a wooden spoon – anything that was handy. I wanted to drown myself in the ditch behind the house.*

> *The billetors stole everything we had – toys and the clothes that fitted their own children.*

> *My sister Anne started to lose her hair and we were getting scabs on our heads and bodies, but they told us to write good things in our letters home.*

> *I was always hungry and had a bad case of worms in my stomach, but I didn't dare tell anyone.*

## ☠ DID YOU KNOW…? ☠

Some people evacuate their dogs to special country pet homes. The dogs are treated well while many of the children have a wuff time.

## Tragic tots

In 1940 evacuees are sent to really safe places overseas. Places like the USA, Canada and Australia. (Well, safe if you can dodge kicking kangaroos and savage sheep.)

But an evacuee ship, The City of Bernares, is sunk by a German submarine on 17 September 1940.

Seventy-three children are drowned and the overseas evacuation plan is ended.

## Tiresome trouble-makers

Children from the cities are sent into the countryside with their teachers. Evacuated. But not all children go. The ones who are left have no schools to go to and nothing to do but make trouble!

Gangs of kids roam the streets and have fun wrecking bomb shelters.

Bomb shelters have to be locked during the day.
Other nuisance games played by bored boys include...

• Collecting baby frogs and throwing them into passing buses full of screaming housewives
• Watching the local army troops practising in the woods. Running up to where one soldier is hiding from the 'enemy' team and shouting, 'He's over here lads!'
• Making bows and arrows from string and wood. Great for scaring cats and dogs
• Making carts from planks and pram wheels then racing down-hill. Old ladies crossing the road make fun targets

## Good games

Stuck in the country? No toys? No shops to shoplift or teachers to torment? Never mind, here are a couple of good games that will REALLY annoy the people around you...

## You need:
A bicycle tyre
A 'Y' shaped tree branch
A boot
A sharp knife

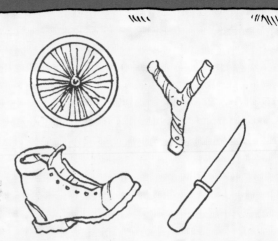

## To Make:
Take the tube out of the tyre and cut it into four – this will make the rubber for the catapult as elastic is in short supply.

Take the tongue from the boot and cut slots in it – this will make the pouch to hold the stones.

Tongue

Slots

Tube

Thread the tube through the slots. Tie an end of the tube to each arm of the tree-branch.

Place a stone in the pouch.

Pull back the pouch as far as it will go.

Take aim and fire!

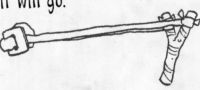

Note: If you can't see a policeman's helmet to aim at, make a nice glass window your target!

There are reports of some policemen smashing boys' catapults and cutting the rubber so they can't fire them.

Spoilsports!

## Summer sledging

ROUND OUR WAY THERE ARE SLAGHEAPS – PILES OF STONE THEY DIG OUT OF THE MINES

ALL YOU NEED IS AN OLD CARDBOARD BOX

CARRY IT TO THE TOP OF THE HILL AND PUT ONE FOOT INTO IT

PUSH OFF AND SLIDE DOWN THE HILL

IF YOU SMASH INTO THE FENCE AT THE BOTTOM THEN PICK UP YOUR TEETH AND SEE WHAT THE TOOTH FAIRY WILL GIVE YOU FOR THEM!

The cardboard soon falls apart, of course. The sledgers find themselves sliding down on ripped trousers and jumpers.

This earns them slaps around the head from angry mothers.

### ☠ DID YOU KNOW...? ☠

Comics are still on sale in the Blitz. You can read all about the man who captures three German submarines all by himself after he knits a chain out of steel. Who is this hero? Desperate Dan, of course. There are also some jolly new war jokes…

Q. WHY DOES HITLER NEVER CHANGE HIS SOCKS?
A. BECAUSE HE SMELLS DEFEAT!

# HORRIBLE HAZARDS

**B**ombs can blow you to bite-sized bits, burn you or bury you. One man described the horror of finding his wife:

> *She was burnt right up to her waist. Her legs were just two cinders ... and her face ... the only way I knew it was her was by one of her boots.*

But bombs cost money. Save those poor Germans the cost. Find other ways to die in the Blitz. Here are ten horribly historical ways that people pop their clogs in Blitzed Britain.

**1 Friendly fire** In 1940 Britain waits for the German invasion. The army decides to have a practice. They send out the code-word 'Cromwell'. That means 'Get ready!'. But SOME dummies think it means the invasion has started.

In Lincolnshire an army team lays land mines across the road to stop German tanks. But their own men are the first to cross it – rushing along the road to join their troop.

Their car is blown to pieces and Lincoln is raining bits of Brits.

**2 Road accidents** In the blackout, road accidents are very common. In November 1941 a policeman, PC William Harold

Story, goes out on his bicycle to make sure everyone gets home safely. He is knocked down by a car and killed.

**3 Alcohol** In 1942 it's hard to find booze in Britain. Some people make their own – it's called 'hooch'. Gangs are busy all over Britain mixing pure alcohol with juniper and almond flavours. Others use methylated spirits. In May 1942 fourteen people die in Glasgow of alcohol poisoning after drinking hooch. Cases like this are reported all over Britain. Many of the victims are soldiers.

HOOCH MAKES HITLER HAPPY

**4 Drowning** It is easy to get lost in the blackout. People who take a wrong turn have been known to step straight off a path and into a canal. Heavy work boots soon drag them down to their death.

But the writer Virginia Woolf decides to kill herself. Her homes in London have been wrecked by bombers and she is miserable. She is depressed. In 1941 she fills her pockets full of stones and walks into a river.

**5 Heart attack** In 1941 in an interview on the radio, the writer Alexander Woollcott is asked about Adolf Hitler. Alex gets so angry he has a heart attack and dies.

There is a dreadful pause while they shift his body from the microphone and put another person there.

**6 Trains** Stations have no lights in the blackout. Many people simply step off the platform, fall on the line and are battered by a tank engine.

If they are knocked out, and no one sees them fall, then death under the wheels of a steam loco is certain.

A man at Hillingdon feels the dark train stop. 'Ah, we must be at Ruislip!' he says. 'I change trains here.'

He steps out of his carriage … and straight off a 30-metre bridge.

A RAIL-LY HORRIBLE WAY TO GO

**7 Grenades** A Home Guard meeting is held to show the men how a No. 68 hand grenade works. It works very well, thank you. It explodes, killing six Home Guard and wounding another 14.

**8 Chilled** When a street has been flattened the fire brigade often has a large concrete tank set in the ground. It's filled with water. Next time there is a large fire they have this great pool of water to put it out.

But these tanks make great swimming pools for kids.

ONE SWIMS AND ONE WAITS AT THE SIDE

THE ONE AT THE SIDE PULLS OUT HIS FRIEND

THEN IT'S HIS TURN

But some dim kids try swimming alone and discover...

You don't, you dummy. You stay there till the cold water kills you.

**9 Pencils** Horrible Histories warning! It's the morning after a bombing raid. If you see a pen or a pencil lying in the street DON'T TOUCH IT!!!

German aircraft have been dropping pens and pencils that will explode when you try to use them!

Remember, the old Horrible Histories joke is not so funny...

**10 Barrage balloons** In London a barrage balloon breaks loose. It falls on the Dover Castle pub and explodes. Two drinkers are killed.

Do they die happy?

## Beautiful balloons

The huge barrage balloons floating in the sky can kill people, but in the Blitz they also save lives.

You have strings on your balloons to stop them flying away. Barrage balloons have steel cables. If an enemy plane flies too low, the steel cables will slice off a wing.

There are accidents ... sometimes British planes fly into the cables!

But that heavy cable can land on people and crush them. So the brainiest Brits have come up with the DPL!

Of course a Horrible Historian will know all about Double Parachute Links, won't you?

That's right ... when an enemy plane hits a cable...

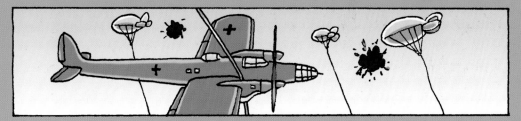

An explosion at each end (a DOUBLE explosion) breaks a LINK, sets the cable free and it drags down the enemy plane…

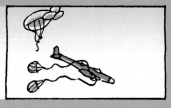

And each cable end has a PARACHUTE on it … when the heavy cable drops it won't fall and smash your skull. It floats down on its parachute.

☠ **DID YOU KNOW…?** ☠

Many Brits believe barrage balloons are huge magnets that suck German planes in and destroy them. (They aren't!)

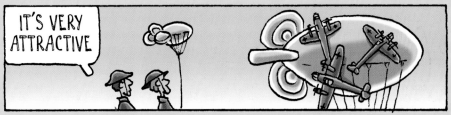

# WOTTEN WORK

Not every fit person can fight in the army, navy or air force. Some have to stay behind and work in the mines and factories.

THAT'S RIGHT! WE CAN'T ALL GO OFF AND GET SHOT AND BLOWN APART!

But there are some jobs no one really wants to do. Jobs like working in a damp, filthy coal mine. So a government minister called Ernest Bevin says…

*We need 720,000 men in this industry. This is where you boys come in. Our fighting men will not be able to win unless we get a good supply of coal.*

No, the soldiers don't want to chuck lumps of coal at the enemy – the coal provides the fuel that makes the steel that makes their guns and tanks.

The 'Bevin Boys' are forced to work in the mines. Their numbers are picked out of a hat – a sort of lottery.

They are given helmets and boots. Bevin Boys aren't given uniforms or badges, they just wear the oldest clothes they can find.

Do the British people say 'Thanks, Bevin Boys?' No, they don't!

• The Bevin Boys are old enough to fight so they are often stopped by police and asked if they are dodging the army.

• The plan goes on until 1948 – three years after the war has finished.

• The Bevin Boys get no medals. They get forgotten.

• No one says a proper 'Thanks' till 50 years after the war in a speech by the Queen … many Bevin Boys are too dead to enjoy the speech.

**Peace protest**

Not everyone wants to fight. If you are an 'objector' you can have a trial.

But in the middle of the Blitz in London you don't always get a fair trial. The judges think you should get out there and fight.

One young objector said…

I AM A CHRISTIAN. I BELIEVE IN PEACE

RUBBISH! EVEN GOD DOESN'T BELIEVE IN PEACE … HE KILLS US ALL IN THE END!

A judge can send you to prison if you refuse to fight (or do a war job, like working in a hospital).

Still, you have to be brave to be an objector. If the judges set you free the Blitzed Brits may decide to beat you up. In some places objectors are thrown into the village pond.

Many are sacked from their jobs.

**Filthy facts**
• Objector Cecil Davies has his picture printed in a newspaper. Someone cuts out the picture, uses it to wipe his bottom, and posts it to Cecil.
• Objectors in the army are given the worst jobs … or weird jobs. Some are told to take a pot of white paint and paint a heap of coal!
• Some objectors let themselves be used for medical tests. One doctor is doing tests for scabies … the mites that cause it are let loose on objectors. Itchy.

# DAD'S DEFENCE

I n 1939 Winston Churchill has one of his bright ideas...

MEN OVER 40 ARE TOO OLD TO JOIN THE ARMY. BUT THEY CAN FORM A HOME GUARD IN CASE MR HITLER'S ARMY LANDS IN BRITAIN

These groups of men are called Local Defence Volunteers (LDV). In July 1940 their name is changed to the Home Guard. But their nickname will always be 'Dad's Army'.

## Things they never tell you about Dad's Army

**1** War starts and Dad's Army have no weapons – the real army need them. So people with guns at home hand them over… One man says he is fighting with gun from 1880.

I'VE A SHOTGUN I USE FOR PIGEONS

I HAVE A PISTOL FROM THE LAST WAR

I'VE GOT A CAP GUN I USE TO SHOOT MY SISTER!

**2** They still don't have enough weapons so they go on parade with…

**Pickaxes ✖ Coshes ✖ Spears ✖ Dummy wooden rifles**

Then Winston Churchill says…

EVERY MAN MUST HAVE A WEAPON – EVEN IF IT IS ONLY A PIKE

Pikes were axes on long poles used in the Middle Ages. Churchill didn't MEAN it. But someone orders metal poles with daggers on the end and a quarter of a million are made.

Dad's Army are furious … they make them look a bit of a joke. Very few of the new 'pikes' ever leave the factory.

**3** You may think the Nazi invaders would treat the LDV as a joke. You're wrong! When Adolf Hitler hears about Dad's Army he rants…

*LDV? They are murder gangs! When we invade they will be rounded up and executed.*

Dad's Army must be pleased to know Adolf is so afraid of them!

**4** The LDV learn to make their own weapons. Weapons like petrol bombs.

TODAY I'M GOING TO SHOW YOU HOW TO MAKE A PETROL BOMB WITH A BEER BOTTLE AND SOME PETROL...

FIRST DRINK THE BEER ... I LIKE THIS BIT...

BOOM!

WHAT WENT WRONG?

HE DRANK THE PETROL

---

### ☠ **DID YOU KNOW...?** ☠

Home-made petrol bombs in Blitzed Britain are known as 'Molotov Cocktails' – but NOT because Mr Molotov invented them.

Molotov was a Russian leader who ordered the Russian army to attack Finland in 1939. The Finns fought back with petrol bombs against Molotov's tanks. They called the bombs Molotov Cocktails.

A Finnish booze factory made half a million of them and sent them to fighters with a matchbox on the side.

**5** Dad's Army is not all made up of older men. There are also boys too young to join the army. These fit young lads make good messengers. To make them even faster what does the LDV give the boys?

    a) Motorbikes

    b) Racing cycles

    c) Roller skates

**Answer:**

c) There is a Home Guard section of 'Skating Boys' who can deliver help quickly by roller-skating to the place they are called!

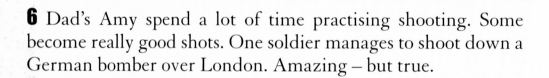

NO TIME TO WAIT, I'VE GOT TO SKATE!

**6** Dad's Amy spend a lot of time practising shooting. Some become really good shots. One soldier manages to shoot down a German bomber over London. Amazing – but true.

**7** Dad's Army are a bit like Boy Scouts. The Home Guard men can earn badges if they pass tests like map-reading and First Aid (which Scouts can do) … and bomb disposal (which Scouts don't do).

YOU'RE JOKING MATE! THAT'S A JOB FOR THE GIRL GUIDES!

**8** The Home Guard also learn how to send signals.
If I ask an LDV man to pass me the Monkey-Orange-Pip Beer-Uncle-Charlie-King-Edward-Tock then he will know exactly what I want!

# THE PHONETIC ALPHABET

| | | | |
|---|---|---|---|
| **A** | Ack | **N** | Nuts |
| **B** | Beer | **O** | Orange |
| **C** | Charlie | **P** | Pip |
| **D** | Don | **Q** | Queen |
| **E** | Edward | **R** | Robert |
| **F** | Freddie | **S** | Sugar |
| **G** | George | **T** | Tock |
| **H** | Harry | **U** | Uncle |
| **I** | Ink | **V** | Vick |
| **J** | Johnnie | **W** | William |
| **K** | King | **X** | X-ray |
| **L** | London | **Y** | Yorker |
| **M** | Monkey | **Z** | Zebra |

## THE PRONUNCIATION OF FIGURES

| | | | |
|---|---|---|---|
| 1 | WUN | 6 | SIX |
| 2 | TOO | 7 | SEV-EN |
| 3 | THR-R-REE | 8 | ATE |
| 4 | FOER | 9 | NINER |
| 5 | FIFE | 0 | OWE |

Try it yourself.

**9** Sometimes you can see your partner but can't hear one another … you might be on hilltops a mile apart. Try 'semaphore signals'…

# THE SEMAPHORE ALPHABET

A 1  B 2  C 3  D 4  E 5

F 6  G 7  H 8  I 9  J

K 0  L  M  N  O

P  Q  R  S  T

U  V  W  X  Y

Z  ATTENTION  NUMERALS FOLLOW  ERROR  READY

**10** The simplest signal of all is to ring the local church bells. It means 'The Germans have landed!'.

But you only do that if you see 25 enemy soldiers or more. Some Dad's Army dopes ring them by mistake and cause a panic.

**Top tip**
And if the Nazis finally land? What can you do?

Boy Scouts are taught how to stretch wire across the road so enemy motorcyclists will be knocked off their bikes. (Unlucky ones would have their heads sliced off.)

But what do you do next?

Don't worry, there is a poster telling you just what to say…

## HOW TO CHALLENGE AN INVADER

**Hands up!**
*Hande hoch!* (Henda hoch)

**Hand over your weapons!**
*Ubergeben sie ihre waffen!*
(Ubergayben zee eerer vuffen)

**Surrender or I shoot!**
*Ergeben sie sich, oder ich schiesse!*
(Aingayben zee zich ohder ich sheesa)

**Quick march!**
*Vorwarts marsch!* (Forvairts marsh)

**Turn round!**
*Umdrehen!* (Oomdrayen)

**Left turn!**
*Links um!* (Links oom)

**Right turn!**
*Rechts um!* (Rechts oom)

That'll teach them. They will throw up their hands and throw down their weapons … or maybe throw down their weapons THEN throw up their hands.

It just goes to show, you can't beat a Blitzed Brit!

**Dad's DIY**

The Home Guard need a few things to help them with their good work ... so the Dads use their DIY skills.

## BARMY BRICKS

Dad's Army learn how to make bricks out of cardboard! These bricks can be scattered over a net to look like rubble from a bombed house.

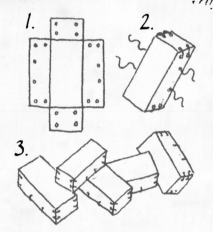

Men with rifles can then hide under the net and shoot at enemy soldiers and surprise them.

Of course if the enemy fire back, the cardboard bricks aren't much help to you.

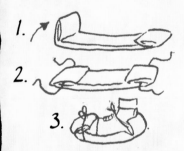

## SNEAKY SACKS

Dad's Army learn to walk silently ... sneak up on the enemy. How do you do this? Make yourself some foot pads from hessian (cloth used to make sack).

But don't just stick your boots in a sack. Oh, no! You need to be taught how to do it properly.

## MAKE-YOUR-OWN PERISCOPE

And Dad's Army even learn to look round corners at the enemy without getting their face blown off.

They are taught how to make periscopes...

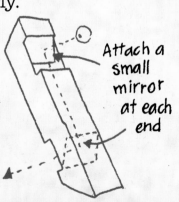

Attach a small mirror at each end

The invasion never comes. If it had then Dad's Army couldn't have stopped it, only slowed it down.

QUICK MARCH? WHO ARE YOU KIDDING?

### ☠ DID YOU KNOW...? ☠

One of the Home Guard working on the anti-aircraft guns has a problem. Every time the gun fires his glass eye drops out.
He is sacked.
So is his mate, a man with no thumbs.

# WOEFUL FOR WOMEN

The women of Britain didn't pick up rifles or find themselves shot at alongside the men, but they suffered in other ways. The ones who stayed in the cities were battered by the Blitz. The ones who went to work saw some sickening sights.

**The return of the Land Army**
In the First World War women had joined 'The Women's Land Army'. They worked mainly on farms, doing men's work while the men went off to fight. Now the Women's Land Army starts again.

The work is just as horrible as ever.

For a healthy, happy job

Join the WOMEN'S LAND ARMY

## Land Army lullaby

The Land Army women have their very own song. Here it is. Sing it till your throat is sore…

### WOMEN'S LAND ARMY SONG

*Back to the land, we must all lend a hand.*
*To the farms and the fields we must go.*
*There's a job to be done,*
*Though we can't fire a gun*
*We can still do our bit with the hoe…*
*Back to the land, with its clay and its sand,*
*Its granite and gravel and grit,*
*You grow barley and wheat*
*And potatoes to eat*
*To make sure that the nation keeps fit…*
*We will tell you once more*
*You can help win the war*
*If you come with us - back to the land.*

Jolly little song. Santa Claus would like it … Hoe! Hoe! Hoe!

Dear Mum

I am getting used to this work at last. I mean, I've seen cows dying, I've pulled a pitchfork from a man's foot, and even helped a man who fell off a hay stack and broke his neck. But I still hate watching a bull have a hole punched in its nose. I just went and hid in the barn.

The one thing I hate most is the rats. Dead ones or live ones. Sometimes I find a dead one when I'm mucking out the cows. They hide in the straw so when the animals lie down they're crushed. There are live rats in the roof of the cottage where I live and I can hear them running up and down all night.

The cow-herd thinks I'm soft. One day the bull refused to eat his food from his trough. We found out why – there were rat droppings in there. We fed the bull from a bucket, and stayed until he had eaten it.

The next day a massive rat appeared from a hole in the wall and started sniffing round the trough.

I ran off in terror to find the cow-herd. We went back to the stall and tiptoed in quietly. Suddenly he reached into the trough, grabbed the rat by its tail, swung it round and smashed its brains out against the door post. He was brilliant!

We've filled in the hole and the rats haven't been back … except in my dreams.

Hope this war ends soon and I can get back to our home in the town.

Lots of love.

Mabel

## Rotten for rats

Not all Land Army women are so scared of rats. In fact many are given the job of rat-catching and they become very good at it.

These rat-catching women don't catch rats by running after them and beating them to death. No. They are a lot sneakier...

On Monday, Tuesday and Wednesday they put down tasty fresh food...

OOOH! DEAD HEDGEHOG ... MY FAVOURITE!

On Thursday they put down *nothing*! That was clever!

AWWW! I'M SO HUNGRY I COULD EAT A HORSE AND ALL FOUR SHOES!

So on Friday, when the catchers put down *poison* food...

TASTES A BIT OFF ... BUT I'M SO HUNGRY I DON'T CARE!

Saturday was the day the women cleared up the poison and the ratty corpses

'JOIN THE WOMEN'S LAND ARMY FOR A HEALTHY, HAPPY JOB!' – UNLESS YOU'RE A RAT!

RAT'S NOT VERY FUNNY!

## Murderous for moles

You notice the Women's Land Army seem to have Thursday as a day off? No they don't. On Thursdays they massacre blind little moles. Why?

One way to kill a mole is to find a molehill and stick a very sharp point down the hole.

But there is a nastier way…

## Gruesome for girls

If you're going to be a Land Girl you need to know that they have accidents like everyone else. Accidents like…

- A tractor belt snaps and cuts a girl to ribbons
- A girl has a finger chopped off in a corn machine
- A woman has her eye poked out with a pitchfork
- A girl saws through her own ankle while cutting wood

## Vile for volunteers

Before the war has even started some women get together and decide to plan. They set up the 'Women's Voluntary Service' (WVS). They will give up their time, without pay, to help anyone who needs it. They…

• Make food and tea for people who've been bombed
• Learn to put out fires
• Knit and sew to make warm clothes for soldiers
• Invent 'Rural Pie Week' and make 70,000 pies for workers in the fields

THE PIE'S THE LIMIT WITH THIS BLOOMIN' LOT!

But they also have some horrible jobs to do … and jobs that the Blitzed Brits don't thank them for!

• When the war starts WVS women knock on doors to ask if people want Anderson shelters for their gardens. They get some very rude replies…

YOU'RE JUST A SCARE-MONGER! THE GERMANS WILL NEVER BOMB COVENTRY. PUSH OFF AND STICK YOUR ANDERSON SHELTER UP YOUR WVS SKIRT!

On 14 November 1940, 500 German bombers drop 500 tons of explosives and around 900 incendiary bombs on Coventry in just ten hours.

Coventry is hit so badly the Germans come up with a new word for flattening cities with bombs – they say they 'Coventrate' them.

The bombs kill 1,200 people in Coventry … but mainly people who had no shelters!

## Awful Auxiliary

• Women can also join the 'Auxiliary Territorial Service' (ATS). Like soldiers, they wear a khaki uniform. But they don't get the exciting jobs. They get the 'housewife' jobs – cooking and cleaning, peeling potatoes and scrubbing floors. Some DO get to work on the anti-aircraft guns. But Winston Churchill says…

• An older WVS woman is put on 'Fire Watch' to listen for enemy bombers and sound the alarm. No one has noticed she is deaf.

# BRAIN BLITZER

Is your brain brilliant? Or is it bomb-blitzed and banjaxed? Try this test on Blitzed Britain. Get more than nought out of ten and you are a Horrible Historian. Get less and you are probably a history teacher...

1 German submarines sink ships going to and from Blitzed Britain. But when they fire a torpedo at the cruise ship Arandora Star in July 1940 they make a big blitzed boob. Why?
a) The Arandora Star is made of rubber — the torpedo bounces back and sinks the German submarine.
b) The Arandora Star is full of Germans, not Blitzed Brits.
c) The Arandora Star is Adolf Hitler's favourite ship — he had cruised on her when he was a boy and he is very cross.

2 You haven't got a shelter and you haven't got a cellar. Bombs are falling. Quick, hide! Where?
a) Under the bed
b) Under the apple tree in the garden
c) Under the stairs

3 Of course the Brits must try to shoot down German bombers. You light up the skies with searchlights. You have barrage balloons on steel ropes to stop the bombers swooping low. You have gunners to fire cannon at them. So which is the most dangerous job?
a) on the searchlight
b) on the balloons
c) on the gun

4 Which Society helps to defeat enemy spies in Blitzed Britain?
a) The Boy Scouts for Freedom Society
b) The Spies and Secret Societies Society
c) The Golf, Cheese and Chess Society

5 A driver is caught speeding. He is driving at over 20 miles an hour at night. What sort of car is it?
a) A police car
b) A hearse carrying a corpse to a funeral
c) A doctor rushing to save a bomb victim

6 What are 'Pig Clubs' in Blitzed Britain?
a) A group of people who 'club' together to buy a piglet
b) Clubs for beating pigs
c) A group of people who dress like pigs to spy on pig farms

7 How can you use beer bottle tops to help the war?
a) Throw them at German bombers
b) Put them back on the beer bottles and save metal
c) Make them into jewellery

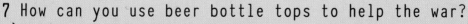

**8** The government says EVERY single work place has to have a fire-watcher on guard at all times — to put out bomb fires as soon as they can. One place catches fire and there is no fire-watcher ready. Which place?
**a)** The Houses of Parliament — so the government breaks its own law
**b)** Buckingham Palace — so the King breaks the law
**c)** Cardiff Fire Station — so the fire station burns down

**9** Two people in a car are killed when they are hit by...?
**a)** A ship
**b)** A chip
**c)** A whip

**10** A man parachutes into your village. How do you check if he is a British pilot or a German?
**a)** Give him a word test — does he speak good English?
**b)** Give him a maths test — cunning Germans can do hard sums, like 37 times 54, in their heads.
**c)** Ask him to name his leader — if he says 'Hitler' shoot him. If he says 'Churchill' give him a cup of tea.

**Answers**

1b) The Arandora Star is a cruise ship, not a warship, so the Germans should not have been firing at her. But she is painted grey so maybe the submarine captain thought it was a warship. The ship was taking German prisoners and German people to Canada. She sinks in 35 minutes. There are 1,500 people onboard and 800 die ... mainly Germans. Ooooops!

2c) Most German houses are built with cellars but Brit houses aren't, so the government says, 'You can always hide under the stairs'. It's good to be German at the start of the war, but later, when German cities are set ablaze by Brit bombers, the cellars become deadly. The fires suck all the air out of the cellars and the families suffocate. Not nice.

3a) If the searchlight can see the bomber then the bomber can see the searchlight. Some enemy aircraft have the job of bombing the searchlights. It's dangerous there, standing next to your searchlight – if the bulb blows then so do you.

4c) The 'Golf, Cheese and Chess Society' is the nickname for GCCS … which is of course the 'Government Code and Cypher School' where spy-catchers learn to crack secret messages.

5b) The undertaker is the first man to be fined for speeding. The corpse is late for her funeral. I don't think she'll mind too much.

6a) A Pig Club is a group of people who 'club' together to buy a piglet. They feed it with all their food scraps. When it is nice and fat they kill it and eat it.

7c) Yes, young ladies really do make jewellery from old beer bottle tops, cup hooks and corks.

8a) On 10 May 1941, a bomb sets fire to the House of Commons. There is no one there to put it out.

Members of Parliament? Or Muppets in Parliament?

9a) … sort of.

When the Malakand is bombed it scatters itself over miles of Liverpool docks. A young couple are driving home along the dock road when bits of the ship land on their car and kill them.

They've just been married. Bride and boom.

10a) Home Guards are given a list of words to see if a parachuting pilot can say them. Try them yourself:

## Soothe   Wrong   Wretch   Rats   Those

One pilot who lands in Wapping, London, fails this test and is beaten to death. But he isn't a German enemy. He is a friendly pilot from Poland.

# FOUL FOOD

Blitzed Britain hardly has enough food to go around. When the government tries to bring in more food in cargo ships the German submarines just sink them.

So the government brings in 'rationing' ... every Brit has a 'ration book' with coupons. Swap your coupons (and your money) for food.

Used up all your coupons? You'll have to go hungry till you get more next week!

**Cruel for coupons**
But it isn't that simple. Some shopkeepers don't have enough for everyone so they just sell to favourite customers...

**Fishy fine**
Restaurants are not allowed to sell meat AND fish to one customer. It is steak or hake, sausage or salmon, turkey or trout ... but not both.

An 'Enforcement Officer' goes into the Odeon Cinema in North London and eats both. Yummy! He then jumps up and says, 'That's against the law! I arrest you!'

The manager and waitresses are all fined. I just hope he paid for his meal.

**Tasty top tips**

As there's not a lot of food to go around you have to eat what you can.

## HORRIBLE HISTORIES NOTE:

This does NOT include next door's dog, your granny's secret supply of mint humbugs, or your gas mask.

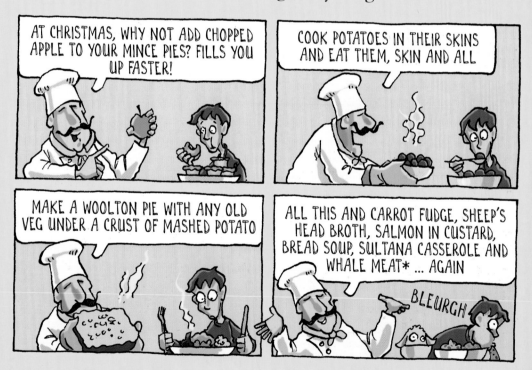

AT CHRISTMAS, WHY NOT ADD CHOPPED APPLE TO YOUR MINCE PIES? FILLS YOU UP FASTER!

COOK POTATOES IN THEIR SKINS AND EAT THEM, SKIN AND ALL

MAKE A WOOLTON PIE WITH ANY OLD VEG UNDER A CRUST OF MASHED POTATO

ALL THIS AND CARROT FUDGE, SHEEP'S HEAD BROTH, SALMON IN CUSTARD, BREAD SOUP, SULTANA CASSEROLE AND WHALE MEAT* ... AGAIN

BLEURGH

This is NOTHING to do with the famous war song, 'Whale meat again'. You are thinking of 'We'll meet again'.

\* Yes, all real war recipes.

A boy said:

*Whale meat tastes like fish. What's wrong with that? So mother soaks it for 24 hours in vinegar. Then it tastes like vinegar. But there's lots of it, so you don't mind!*

## Dig for victory

Still hungry? Then why not grow your own food? Posters have snappy verses to get you started…

DIG FOR VICTORY

Dig! Dig! Dig! And your muscles will grow big
Keep on pushing the spade
Don't mind the worms
Just ignore their squirms
And when your back aches laugh with glee
And keep on diggin'
Till we give our foes a Wiggin'
Dig! Dig! Dig! to Victory!

Never mind the worms? That's easy to say if you're not a worm!

**Doctor Carrot**

The good news is there are plenty of carrots to eat! So you need top tips on how to cook and eat (and drink) them!

'Doctor Carrot' is a cartoon character who can help. Try his real recipes and top tips.

### HORRIBLE HISTORIES NOTE:

Don't blame me if you end up looking like Doctor Carrot!

# CURRIED CARROTS
### *(for 4 people)*

**YOU WILL NEED:**
Carrots, 25g margarine or dripping, 1½ teaspoonfuls curry powder, 1 onion, ½ pint water, 3 teaspoonfuls flour, salt and pepper, rice

**METHOD**
Chop the carrots and boil for ten minutes.
Make the curry sauce while the carrots boil.

Melt the fat in a pan. Add chopped onion and fry for a few minutes.
Add curry powder and flour and fry for a few minutes.
Stir in water and bring to the boil.
Simmer gently for about 30 minutes.

Add cooked carrots to curry sauce in saucepan and cook for another 20 to 30 minutes.
Serve with cooked rice.

Mmmm! Disgusting or what?

DON'T FANCY IT? NEVER MIND, YOU CAN TRY CARROT JAM OR HOME-MADE POP CALLED CARROLADE (MADE FROM THE JUICES OF CARROTS AND TURNIPS!)

I THINK I'D RATHER EAT MY DAD'S SOCKS, THANKS

## Potato Pete

Doctor Carrot's cartoon mate is Potato Pete. Guess what he looks like? (If you answer 'A big red bus', then you probably need to see a doctor – a brain doctor, not a Carrot Doctor.)

Yes, Potato Pete is a potato man. He not only has his own songs, he even changes nursery rhymes so titchy toddlers get the message too!

Here are some of his rotten rhymes…

*Little Jack Horner*
*Sat in a corner*
*Eating potato pie.*
*He took a large bite,*
*And said with delight,*
*Oh, what a strong boy am I.*

*Jack Spratt could eat no fat*
*His wife could eat no lean;*
*So they both ate potatoes*
*And scraped their platters clean.*

PATHETIC!

*There was an old woman who lived in a shoe.*
*She had so many children she didn't know what to do.*
*She gave them potatoes instead of some bread,*
*And the children were happy and very well fed.*

Horrible Histories readers can do better, can't you? Have a go…

GEORGIE PORGY PUDDING AND CHIPS?

JACK AND JILL WENT UP THE HILL TO FETCH A PAIL OF POTATOES?

LITTLE MISS MUFFET SAT ON A PLATE OF MASH?

OLD MOTHER HUBBARD WENT TO THE CUPBOARD TO GET HER POOR DOGGIE A SPUD?

'THREE BLIND POTATOES, SEE HOW THEY RUN.' WHY WERE THEY BLIND? THEY HAD NO EYES. HUH! POTATOES, EYES, GEDDIT?

YES, BUT I WISH I HADN'T!

### Winning the scraps

From August 1940 it is against the law to waste food. You can go to prison for a dumped dumpling or making a fritter litter.

A café called Lyons is fined for wasting sandwiches. What has happened to their sandwiches?

Mice have eaten them!

MMMM! CHEESE. MY FAVOURITE!

Waste NOTHING is the message. If it's too disgusting to eat then put it in a bin.

### HORRIBLE HISTORIES NOTE:

If you put GOOD food in the pig bins you will be punished! There are Pig Bin Inspectors who check the bins. They even hide and spy on some bins to catch food wasters. Nice job to have.

Now find a pig to feed your old food to. That's the way to win the war, the poem says…

*Because of the pail, the scraps were saved,*
*Because of the scraps, the pigs were saved,*
*Because of the pigs, the rations were saved,*
*Because of the rations, the ships were saved,*
*Because of the ships, the island was saved,*
*Because of the island, the Empire was saved,*
*And all because of the housewife's pail.*

A jolly poster shows happy pigs spelling out 't-h-a-n-k-s'.

See those extra two pigs? They probably know what will happen when they are fed and fat…

I reckon the extra pigs have 'n-o' on their backs.

☠ **DID YOU KNOW…?** ☠

Doctor Carrot and Potato Pete have other friends with helpful hints. Mrs Sew-and-sew will tell you how to make clothes from curtains.

They probably look awful…

There is also the ugly 'Squander Bug' … a nasty Nazi beetle who wants you to waste your money in the shops.

(Seventy years after the war there are still Squander Bugs around.)

**Nag your butcher**

There is not a lot of meat about. Some butchers seem to have a bit extra. They will sell you lots of tasty beef for a nice hot meal. Yummy!

Except it isn't beef … it is horse meat. More like a nice trot meal. Some will even sell you diseased meat. Yeuch.

## Savage salvage

It isn't just food that can be saved. Pots and pans can be handed over to make aeroplanes. As one happy poster poem says…

MY SAUCEPANS HAVE ALL BEEN SURRENDERED,
THE TEAPOT IS GONE FROM THE HOB,
THE FRYING PAN'S LEAVING THE BACON,
FOR A VERY MUCH DIFFERENT JOB.
SO NOW, WHEN I HEAR THE WIRELESS
OF HURRICANES SHOWING THEIR METTLE,
I SEE IN A VISION BEFORE ME …
A GERMAN PLANE CHASED BY MY KETTLE.

# CRUEL CRIME

The Second World War ends in 1945. But the war against crime never stops, never will.

In Blitzed Britain the crimes do change a little.

### Blitz baddies

Teen gangs roam during the blackout and fight. They are a real problem during the early years of the war. In one fight James Harvey is beaten to death by a rival gang near the Elephant and Castle Underground station. He's just 17 years old.

His attackers get between one and three years in jail. Why not life?

Some people use the blackout to attack policemen on the street. In one attack TWO policemen are badly beaten by an attacker who hits them with a gas mask. Who is this thug? Mary Maher, aged 35, from Ireland.

### Lots of lovely loot

• If a house is bombed then why not pop in and pinch whatever you can? This is called 'looting'. The law says looters CAN be hanged or shot for this … but they never are.

> WELL, THEY'RE PROBABLY DEAD. WON'T MISS THE STUFF WILL THEY?

• In the first months of the Blitz there are 400 cases of looting … and that's just the ones who were caught. TWENTY of these are firemen. 'We make a splash then take your cash!'

• Chief Inspector Percy Datlen tells what happened in Dover after one bombing raid:

> *In one street, the looters have gone through the lot. Carpets have been stripped from the floors, stair carpets have been removed: they have even taken away heavy mangles, bedsteads and complete suites of furniture.*

Looting is hard work!

 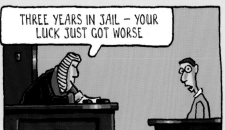

## 🕱 DID YOU KNOW…? 🕱

There is a lot of Blitz fraud. If your house is bombed then the government will pay for repairs and clothes and furniture. But there are too many to keep a check. One man, Walter Handy, is arrested …

> YOU SAID YOU WERE BOMBED OUT 19 TIMES IN 9 WEEKS!

> YEAH … WELL I WAS UNLUCKY WASN'T I?

> THREE YEARS IN JAIL – YOUR LUCK JUST GOT WORSE

## Blackout baddies

• Bomb shelters are great places for nicking someone's things when they fall asleep. And when people crowd in you can pick a pocket or lift a bag.

• Here's a dangerous one. Wait till the air-raid warning siren sounds. People run from their houses to their garden shelters or the street shelters. While they are gone, go and burgle their houses. (Of course bombs may fall on you but that's a chance you have to take.)

• The Home Guard ('Dad's Army') can be careless with their weapons. Seven teenage boys steal three machine guns from a Home Guard store in North London. They hold up 43 shops and cinemas before they are caught.

• A top tip for car drivers. In the blackout knock a woman cyclist off her bike and pinch her handbag. American soldier Karl Hulten tries this in 1944 and gets away with it. When he starts murdering women for their money he is caught and hanged.

• Murder in the dark is easier. In February 1942 four women are murdered in the blackout. One has been attacked with a tin opener. Some worried people fear Jack the Ripper is back...

But the careless Ripper drops his gas mask when he attacks his next victim. It has his name inside! He is RAF Cadet Gordon Cummings and he is arrested and hanged.

☠ **DID YOU KNOW...?** ☠

A tin opener is a useful tool. A London rescue centre is given hundreds of cans of soup for the homeless ... but no opener.
A job for the Blackout Ripper, perhaps?

### Teen terrors

Just a year after the war started all the prisons for boys (remand homes) are full! War time is crime-time for teens. Some are punished with a beating with a bundle of birch twigs. What do these young villains do?

They...

• Break windows
• Smash light bulbs on trains
• Damage plants in parks
• Slash cinema seats

And worse ... two boys break out of a remand home in South London and steal a machine gun, but are caught before they can blast the bobbies.

# Krafty killing

There are more murders happening in the Blitz. Why? Because people think they can 'lose' the corpses among all the bomb-blast victims. Take the case of Harry Dobkin.

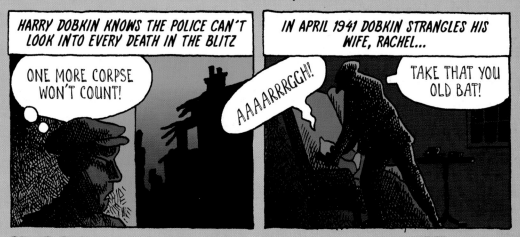

HARRY DOBKIN KNOWS THE POLICE CAN'T LOOK INTO EVERY DEATH IN THE BLITZ

ONE MORE CORPSE WON'T COUNT!

IN APRIL 1941 DOBKIN STRANGLES HIS WIFE, RACHEL...

AAAARRRGGH!

TAKE THAT YOU OLD BAT!

HE COVERS HER IN LIME AND BURIES HER UNDER THE RUIN OF A BOMBED CHURCH...

IT'S LIME CRIME TIME!

BUT DOPEY DOBKIN DOESN'T KNOW LIME STOPS A BODY FROM ROTTING

THE MURDERER SHOULD HAVE USED QUICK LIME ... NOT THE SAME THING AT ALL. QUICK LIME MAKES BODIES ROT

WHEN RACHEL'S BODY IS FOUND DOCTORS DISCOVERED SHE'D BEEN STRANGLED

YOU'RE NICKED!

LOOKS LIKE I'M IN FOR A LONG STRETCH

HE WAS HANGED

A LONG STRETCH OF THE NECK!

## Bleak black market

Some people are prepared to sell you stuff WITHOUT rationing coupons … but you have to pay a lot more!

This secret market is called the 'black market' and it is against the law. Men who run the black market are often known as 'spivs'.

Where do the spivs get their meat, petrol, sugar and clothes?

SOMETIMES WE JUST PINCHES THEM! WE STEALS VEGETABLES FROM PEOPLE'S GARDENS. MUDDY HARD WORK!

AND SOMETIMES WE BUYS THEM FROM PEOPLE WHAT HAS A BIT EXTRA! A FARMER WITH A DEAD COW

SOMETIMES WE PAYS A LORRY DRIVER TO LET US NICK HIS LOAD

The Member of Parliament Joseph Clynes says …

*The black market is wrecking our war effort so it is treason. The men should be flogged with a cat o'nine tails.*

CAT O'NINE TAILS? I CAN SELL YOU A VERY NICE ONE, THREE POUNDS AND CHEAP AT HALF THE PRICE

A good spiv trick is to sell new clothes without coupons.

Just say they are 'second-hand'. A second-hand suit can be sold without coupons.

The open-air market at Romford is a good place to go for this dodge.

## Crafty coupon catchers

Coupons are like money, so of course there are people out to nick them.

A coupon officer in Brighton phones the police…

The books have gone and the coupon officer isn't much help. She can't say when they were taken or how the thieves got in.

Then police hear that stolen ration books are for sale in a pub. They send along a policeman in plain clothes to buy a stolen book.

As soon as the policeman has bought a stolen book he arrests the seller.

The policeman takes her to the station where he doesn't crack any old jokes like these...

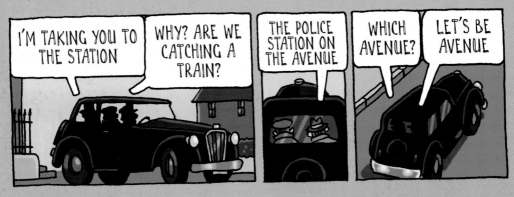

And when they get her to the station (without the jokes) they discover she is...

Yes, she'd stolen her own supplies.

A sad story but it happens all the time ... shop assistants nick knickers, office workers nick notepads and teachers pinch pens.

# AWFUL FOR ALIENS

If you are foreign – or if your parents were foreign – then Blitzed Brits don't trust you.

After all, you could be a spy.

In 1930 there had been 20,000 Germans living in Britain. By 1939 there are 60,000 – many people who've run away from the nasty Nazis in Germany.

These foreign people are called 'aliens'. And life for aliens can be tough.

• Aliens can be thrown out of their jobs for no reason. (King George VI's royal family are German, of course, but no one throws HIM out of his job!)

• In May 1940 Churchill decides to have many of the aliens locked away. To keep Britain safe, he says...

*Collar the lot!*

• Many aliens are kept in 'internment' camps which are not at all like holiday camps. They sleep in tents without mattresses and with only earwigs for company. They are not allowed newspapers, radios or letters.

• In Germany the Nazis are killing the Jewish people they hate. In Britain many Nazis are 'interned' along with Jews! The Nazis like to terrify the Jews at night by singing songs like...

WHEN THE BLOOD OF JEWS GUSHES FROM OUR KNIVES, THEN THE WORLD WILL BE TWICE AS GOOD

• Over 7,000 aliens are sent to cold Canada where they can't harm the Brit fight. They are crammed into ships and packed off. (A bit like slave ships all over again.) The Duke of Devonshire says...

*We need to save our food for Britain and get rid of useless mouths and so forth.*

• Some aliens are made to work on the land (like slaves). But some are given a much trickier job ... making unexploded bombs safe.

## Shooting spies

Of course SOME foreign people in Britain really ARE spies. Poor Karel Richter was a spy … but not a very good one!

RICHTER DROPPED INTO BRITAIN ON A PARACHUTE AND HID FOR TWO DAYS WITHOUT FOOD...

DON'T FEEL SO HOT!

THAT MADE HIM SO ILL HE WENT FOR HELP. TWO LORRY DRIVERS FOUND HIM WANDERING IN THE ROAD...

WATCH OUT YOU CLOT!

THEY HANDED HIM OVER TO THE BRIT SPY-CATCHERS...

IT'S ALL A PLOT

RICHTER'S RADIO AND GUN WERE FOUND IN THE FIELD WHERE HE LANDED

YES, HERE'S THE SPOT!

HE OWNED UP

I CONFESS THE LOT!

...AND THE BRITISH EXECUTED HIM

NOW I'VE BEEN SHOT!

# EPILOGUE

Wars can be horribly cruel. The worst wars kill women and children who aren't even fighting. Wars can get SO cruel even the killers get sick of the slaughter and tired of the torture.

That's what happened in the early 1300s in Berwick. King Edward I of England told his men to slaughter the Scots in the town of Berwick.

Reports said that 11,000 men, women and children were butchered. Then Edward saw a woman giving birth to a baby. One of Ed's soldiers slaughtered them both. Edward was sickened.

But the Second World War was different. Death dropped from the sky. Men could massacre with bombs and they didn't have to see the suffering. It was the people on the ground who saw what the brutal bombs did to babies as well as children, women and old people.

A man in Belfast told one of the most horribly historical tales ever…

AFTER ONE BOMB RAID I SAW A STARVING ALSATIAN DOG WITH A DEAD BABY IN ITS MOUTH. IT WAS RUNNING OFF. I TOOK OFF MY METAL HELMET AND THREW IT ONTO THE RUBBLE. THE CLATTER SCARED THE DOG AND IT DROPPED THE BABY. I WENT TO A BOMBED HOUSE AND PULLED OUT SOME TATTERED NET CURTAIN. I WRAPPED THE BABY'S BODY IN IT. I FOUND SOME SOLDIERS AND LEFT THE BABY WITH THEM. WE FASTENED A NOTE TO THE LITTLE BODY SAYING IT WAS FOUND ON YORK STREET. YOU NEVER FORGET THINGS LIKE THAT. NEVER.

The pilots who dropped the bomb that killed the baby didn't see the pitiful death. The Blitzed Brits knew there was just one way to SHOW the enemy the horror of the Blitz … do it to THEM.

So the RAF and the United States Air Force began to flatten German cities and kill more innocent people.

So Hitler told his scientists to make flying bombs – 'Revenge' weapons – that would bring a new Blitz to Britain.

And so it went on.

That's why more people died in the Second World War than in any other war. Bigger and nastier bombs, till it all ended with two massive atomic bombs dropped on Japan.

At Hiroshima a single atomic bomb killed more people than died in the Blitz in six years.

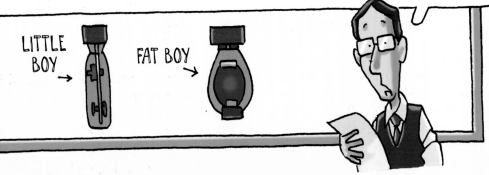

ON 6 AUGUST 1945 THE BOMB CALLED 'LITTLE BOY' WAS DROPPED ON HIROSHIMA. IT KILLED 70,000 PEOPLE. OVER THE NEXT FEW MONTHS, ANOTHER 60,000 DIED FROM INJURIES OR POISONING. THREE DAYS LATER, AT NAGASAKI ANOTHER 70,000 WERE KILLED BY A BOMB CALLED 'FAT MAN'

LITTLE BOY →

FAT BOY →

Two bombs ... 200,000 deaths.
The whole of the Blitz on Britain ... 60,595 deaths.
We live in a world of weapons like that.

THERE WILL BE NO MORE BLITZES NOW

# INTERESTING INDEX

Hang on! This isn't one of your boring old indexes. This is a horrible index. It's the only index in the world where you will find exploding pencils, massacred moles, squirmy worms and all the other things you really HAVE to know if you want to be a horrible historian. Read it and creep.

Terry Deary was born at a very early age, so long ago he can't remember. But his mother, who was there at the time, says he was born in Sunderland, north-east England, in 1946 – so it's not true that he writes all *Horrible Histories* from memory. At school he was a horrible child only interested in playing football and giving teachers a hard time. His history lessons were so boring and so badly taught, that he learned to loathe the subject. *Horrible Histories* is his revenge.

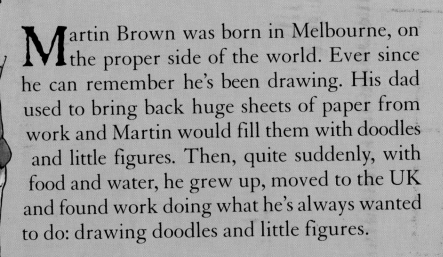

Martin Brown was born in Melbourne, on the proper side of the world. Ever since he can remember he's been drawing. His dad used to bring back huge sheets of paper from work and Martin would fill them with doodles and little figures. Then, quite suddenly, with food and water, he grew up, moved to the UK and found work doing what he's always wanted to do: drawing doodles and little figures.